Contents

INTRODUCTION

Plumbing is a trade with many intricacies. Many problem solving techniques have to be learned because, in most properties, additional plumbing is added to existing systems to create new shower installations, new en-suite toilets, additional sinks, bathrooms and basins.

Washing machines and dishwashers are plumbed in by non experts and outside taps are fitted sometimes with no regard for regulations regarding non return valves. These can all cause problems from a badly jointed U bend to a piece of pipe that has been capped off and collects air causing a "dead leg" and air lock.

Basic plumbing is something everyone should try. As long as you know how to turn all your water valves off you can stay safe and dry!

In a new home, the plumbing system features three main components, the water supply system, the drainage system, and the appliance/fixture set.

In most communities, to install plumbing, you must be a licensed plumber, or you must work under a licensed plumber who approves and oversees your work. Local codes determine standard plumbing procedures, but a new home's fixture placement, pipe routing layout, and pipe size depend on the home's design.

Sewer accommodation stubs are set before pouring the concrete foundation, but the bulk of the plumbing takes place later. The rough-in plumbing phase, which occurs in conjunction with the wiring and duct installation phase, takes place after the framing is complete, but before hanging drywall. This is the time to install main drains in floors and connect them to the stack. Rough-in drain fittings install now for sinks and tubs. This is also the time to install water supply pipes or tubing and set toilet flanges.

Because they're often too large to set once walls and doorways are framed, tubs and tub/shower units are typically set before framing the walls. Since a lot of construction has yet to take place, cover these fixtures with cardboard or even old blankets or rugs to protect them from scratches. Set and connect sinks and commodes last, after finishing the walls and laying the flooring.

CHAPTER ONE

Plumbing follows the basic laws of nature -- gravity, pressure, water seeking its own level. Knowing this, you can understand its "mysteries" and make dozens of fixes to your home's plumbing system. You can save yourself time, trouble, and money!

The plumbing system in your home is composed of two separate subsystems. One subsystem brings freshwater in, and the other takes wastewater out. The water that comes into your home is under pressure. It enters your home under enough pressure to allow it to travel upstairs, around corners, or wherever else it's needed. As water comes into your home, it passes through a meter that registers the amount you use. The main water shutoff, or stop, valve is typically located close to the meter. In a plumbing emergency, it's vital that you quickly close the main shutoff valve. Otherwise, when a pipe bursts, it can flood your house in no time. If the emergency is confined to a sink, tub, or toilet, however, you may not want to turn off your entire water supply. Therefore, most fixtures should have individual stop valves.

Water from the main supply is immediately ready for your cold water needs. The hot water supply, however, requires another step. One pipe carries water from the cold water system to your water heater. From the heater, a hot water line carries the heated water to all the fixtures, out-lets, and appliances that require hot water. A thermostat on the heater maintains the temperature you select by turning the device's heating elements on and off as required. The normal temperature setting for a home water heater is between 140 degrees F and 160 degrees F, but 120 degrees F is usually adequate and is also more economical. Some automatic dishwashers require higher temperature water, though many of these have a water heater within them that boosts the temperature another 20 degrees F.

Whether your home is on a sewer or septic system, the systems within your home are essentially the same. Drainage systems do not depend on pressure, as supply systems do. Instead, waste matter leaves your house because the drainage pipes all pitch, or angle, downward. Gravity pulls the waste along. The sewer line continues this downward flow to a sewage treatment facility or a septic tank.

Traps are vital components of the drainage system. You can see a trap under every sink. It is the curved or S-shape section of pipe under a drain. Water flows from the basin with enough force to go through the trap and out through the drainpipe, but enough water stays in the trap afterward to form a seal that prevents sewer gas from backing up into your home. Every fixture must have a trap. Toilets are self-trapped and don't require an additional trap at the drain. Bathtubs frequently have drum traps, not only to form a seal against sewer gas but also to collect hair and dirt in order to prevent clogged drains. Some kitchen sinks have grease traps to collect grease that might otherwise cause clogging. Because grease and hair are generally the causes of drain clogs, traps often have clean-out plugs that give you easier access to remove or break up any blockage.

Since a drainage system involves all of these components, it is usually referred to as the DWV: the drain-waste-vent system. If water is to flow out freely and waste is to exit properly, all components of the DWV must be present and in good working order. Examine the pipes in the basement or crawl space under your house to help you understand the system better.

Supply and Drainage Subsystems

The supply and drainage subsystems are two distinct operations, with no overlapping between them. There are bridges between the two, however, and the bridges are what make the plumbing system worth having. In plumbing jargon, any bridge between the supply and drainage systems is a fixture.

Toilets, sinks, and tubs are fixtures. In addition, an outside faucet is a fixture and so is a washing machine. All devices that draw freshwater and discharge wastewater are fixtures, and all are designed to keep the supply and drainage systems strictly segregated.

Some fixtures have individual supply shutoff valves so you don't need to close the main shutoff to repair them. It's a good idea to make sure everyone in the family knows the location of the main shutoff valve in your house as well as how to use it. You may want to tag the main shutoff valve so anyone can easily find it.

Before you embark on any plumbing repairs, always turn off the water supply to the fixture or the main shutoff. In addition, check with your local plumbing code official before you add or change any pipe in your house. You will learn what is allowed and what is prohibited and whether or not a homeowner is allowed to do his or her own work. If you get the green light, you can save yourself a lot of money by doing your own repairs.

Hard Water and How It Damages Plumbing

The term hard water is used to describe a fresh water supply that contains relatively high amounts of natural minerals calcium and magnesium and a variety of trace metals. Hard water is not bad for your health, but it can cause problems in plumbing and appliances and is considered a nuisance by many homeowners. Understanding exactly what hard water is and how it affects your plumbing can help you determine what, if anything, needs to be done about it.

How Does Water Become Hard?

Although rainwater is pure when it falls from the sky, as it flows from the surface into aquifers, it absorbs minerals, primarily calcium and magnesium. This absorption changes it from soft to hard water. The amount of mineral content that water contains determines the hardness level of the water. Water hardness is commonly measured in milligrams per liter (mg/L) or grains of mineral per gallon (GPG). The United States Geological Survey (USGS) measures water hardness as milligrams of calcium carbonate per liter of water and classifies hardness levels as follows:

• 0 to 60 mg/L: Soft

• 61 to 120 mg/L: Moderately hard

• 121 to 180 mg/L: Hard

• More than 181 mg/L: Very hard

Common Problems

Hard water can be problematic because it reacts with cleaning products, creates soap buildup, and can wear down fixtures and appliances more quickly than soft water. The minerals in hard water react with soap to create soap scum, inhibiting suds. This means you need to use more soap with hard water. The buildup of minerals on glasses and dishes, clothing, fixtures, and even skin and hair can take their toll over time. Here are some of the common household problems related to hard water:

• Scale buildup inside water supply pipes, restricting water flow

• Film and scale buildup on ceramic tile and fixtures

• Difficulty rinsing off soap and shampoo completely, leaving skin or hair feeling dry or dull

• Scale deposits shortening the life of water heaters

• Spots on glasses and dishes cleaned in dishwater

• Less effective clothes washing due to lack of suds

• Increased wear on clothing during washing

What Does It Do to Plumbing?

The buildup on tubs, shower, sinks, and faucets caused by hard water are only part of the problem. The minerals in hard water also start to build up inside pipes, fixtures, and appliances over time. The build-up we don't see can start to cause all sorts of plumbing problems, such as reduced water flow, clogs, and increased stress on pipes and fixtures. The mineral deposits can also cause appliances to operate less efficiently and wear down faster. For example, a water heater has to heat all of the mineral scale buildup inside the tank, as well as the water. Overall, hard water can result in less efficient plumbing and more repairs over time.

Testing for Hard Water

White scale buildup on plumbing fixtures is often a good indicator of the presence of hard water. If you suspect that you have hard water, there is a low-tech way to test for it by shaking up a small amount of dish soap and water in a closed container. If the solution fails to create lots of suds, you probably have hard water. For much more precise results you can contact your water provider and request a recent water testing report. You can also have a sample of your water tested at a local lab or have a company perform an on-site test (just watch out for conflict of interest; for example, you don't want a test done by a water softener company). Another option is to use a water hardness test strip (sold at home centers and hardware stores) that you hold under running water then match to a color gauge.

Solutions

Water-conditioning products are available and can be used for dealing with mildly hard water. However, the most complete and common solution for treating hard water is a whole-house water softener. Installing a water softener system in cases where the water tests above 3 GPG is often the most effective and efficient solution.

Improving Water Quality in Your Home

Several issues can contribute to discoloration or funny taste of your tap water. Most of these causes are related to what is happening on your property or in your city. Thankfully, you can take steps to improve your drinking water, no matter where you live.

On City Water

City water homes can be a little more certain that water problems originate on your property. However, some exceptions exist, like Flint, Michigan, where lead contamination was found in the municipal system.

Begin by evaluating your pipes. In addition to noticeable changes in color and taste, changes in water pressure can also be a sign of issues. Corrosion can cause a partial blockage within pipes. You can also check the exterior of your pipes, looking for leaks.

Note that pipe repairs or replacements are often best left to a professional unless you are an experienced DIYer.

On Well Water

The first step to improving well water is to have it tested to find out if contaminants are present. If the water is clean, then you should investigate other issues such as leaks. If you do unearth a chemical imbalance, there are water treatments that may make a difference.

Check the pump and well casing for cracks or leaks. These can lead to seals failing and water becoming contaminated with dirt and sediment. Hiring a professional can ensure you get any fixes made properly.

Water Filtration Systems

Whether you're on city or well, a water filtration system can remove impurities and improve the taste. Depending on what solution you choose, the cost can range from $15 to 20 for a faucet purifier or thousands for a whole-home system. More than 2,000 surveyed homeowners invested an average of $1,700 on their filtering system.

The first step to improving your home's water quality is to find out which system will work best for your household.

Whole-House Filters

This filters all the water you use, including that for showers and laundry. Typically, whole-house purifiers are installed on the main water supply line and may involve both a pre-filter and the main system. In most cases, they should be installed by professional plumbers.

Point-of-Entry Filters

If your water is generally fine but sometimes has an objectionable color, odor or taste, then a purifier installed on the cold-water supply line that comes into your sink or refrigerator can help. These are usually smaller and can be done by a homeowner with moderate plumbing knowledge and a pipe cutter and wrench. Some purifiers can be installed directly on the kitchen faucet.

Reverse Osmosis Systems

Reverse osmosis systems are usually installed at the sink, but faucet models are also available. These work by passing the water through a series of membranes that remove bacteria, sediment, and pollutants. Oxygen and some naturally occurring minerals stay behind, allowing for good-tasting drinking water. The complexity of the system makes it best installed by a professional, but you'll need to replace the filters on a regular schedule.

Distillers

These systems remove all the impurities from water, including minerals and oxygen. They heat the water to create steam, then condense it into pure water. Distillers are not as tricky to install, and many homeowners will be able to connect them without hiring a professional.

But if your issues are largely cosmetic and are not health hazards, changing your pipes, checking your well and considering a water filtration or purification system may help you get clean, refreshing water.

Common Plumbing Mistakes That Homeowners Make

Lots of people like to do their own plumbing work, either to save money or because they enjoy tinkering around the house. While there's something to be said for doing one's own plumbing work, these common mistakes can have expensive results. Knowing the pitfalls of doing your own plumbing work, and how to avoid those pitfalls can help you take care of your home.

Use of Chemical Drain Cleaner

For many homeowners, a liquid drain cleaner seems like a miracle product. Just a few cups of chemicals down your drain can open the pipes and send wastewater into the sewer. Unfortunately, chemical drain cleaners can have a lasting effect on galvanized plumbing. People who use this product regularly could cause their pipes to become corroded and leaky.

There are many ways to clear clogs without releasing caustic chemicals into your home's plumbing. Alternative products include:

▢ **Plumbing Auger**: This manually powered device is similar to a drain snake and cleans most drain clogs without a plumber or caustic chemicals.

▢ **Natural Products:** To clear a slow drain, sprinkle it with baking soda, then pour in vinegar and leave the solution to sit for several hours. When you're done, flush it with hot water.

If none of this works, call a plumber. A good plumber can clear the clogs in your drains without using harsh chemicals that could damage your home's plumbing.

Forgetting to Turn Off the Water

You'll need to do this for most water-related projects. Failure to turn off the water before beginning a plumbing improvement or repair can lead to gushing pipes, a small household flood, or a terrible mess. Get to know your home's plumbing before beginning your next plumbing project. Turn off the water at the local shutoff valve. If you can't find that, turn it off at the water main.

Performing Unpermitted Work

Homeowners who make significant changes to their home's plumbing without pulling the proper permits could devalue their home. Homes with unpermitted work may take longer to sell and may sell for less money.

Some states require contractors to pull permits, and others allow homeowners to pull permits themselves. Either way, homeowners must make sure that permits are pulled whenever they perform major work like installation of a bathroom or repiping. Permits enable local building officials to have oversight over home improvement projects. This helps ensure that every home improvement project in the community is performed to code. Although getting a permit can cost money up front, a permit can protect you from fines down the road while also ensuring that your plumbing work is done properly.

Connecting Galvanized and Copper Pipes

When galvanized and copper pipes are allowed to touch one another, corrosion is the result. Many homeowners who do their own plumbing work are unaware of this problem and will repair galvanized piping with modern copper pipes. This can be done if a special piece, called a dielectric union, is used. The dielectric union is a special joint that uses a plastic sleeve and rubber washer to prevent the copper and galvanized piping from touching one another.

DIYing Without Proper Training

Some homeowners take plumbing challenges without getting a license or insurance (which most professionals can provide). Pros know all about how home plumbing works. They go through vocational training to learn about proper drainage and the best equipment. They complete an apprenticeship and gain years of experience before taking a licensing exam. All this experience and expertise ensures the quality of the project and safety of your home.

Taking on a home improvement project that's over your head could result in damage to your home. Doing DIY work without knowledge of the process can also cost more money in the future if you're required to pay a contractor to redo your work later.

Sometimes it's hard to tell when a project is beyond your skill level. The best way to find out is to consult with plumbers before beginning a project. Ask questions like, "how would you do this?" and "what is involved in completing this project?" Talking to experts can help you gauge how complex a project is and whether you have the skills and tools to do the job.

Useful Tools and Materials for Plumbing Projects

While professional plumbers drive around with plenty of specialty equipment on their trucks, homeowners can handle more of their own needs with just a handful of plumbing tools. This is because the most common household plumbing repairs are more about the know-how (and replacement parts) than about advanced tools and special techniques. But there are a few specialty items that are indispensable for everyday plumbing jobs. Topping the list are those for the most familiar plumbing problems of all: clogged drains.

Sink Auger

A sink auger (also called a drum auger or canister auger) is the ultimate weapon for breaking up and clearing clogs in sink and tub drains. Just don't use it on toilets—they call for a closet auger or toilet auger.

A sink auger consists of a flexible stainless steel cable with a corkscrew tip at the end. The cable is coiled within a drum canister and is extended into a drain to reach a clog and clear it. The drum has a handle, and there's a thumbscrew that locks the cable to the canister, and when you insert the cable into the drain and turn the handle, the rotating drum snakes the cable through bends in the drain pipe, allowing the cable tip to penetrate clogs and pull them out.

Toilet or Closet Auger

The toilet auger (also called a closet auger or water closet auger) is used to clear clogs in toilets. You do not want to use a sink auger for toilets, or toilet auger for standard drains, as the tools are designed for very different purposes. A toilet auger has a long metal rod with a bend for reaching into the hole at the bottom of the toilet bowl. A rubber sleeve covers the bend to protect the porcelain in the toilet from being scratched. Once the tool is in place, you push and rotate the auger cable to snake it into or through the clog.

Flange Plunger (Toilet Plunger)

The flange plunger, or ball or toilet plunger, is a specially shaped plunger used to clear clogs in toilets. It works like a regular plunger but has a flange—an extended rubber flap below the dome of the plunger head—that helps seal around the hole at the bottom of the toilet bowl. With the bottom opening sealed, the plunger can effectively create the hydraulic pressure necessary to dislodge most clogs from a toilet.

Cup Plunger (Sink and Tub Plunger)

The cup plunger may be the most common plumbing tool in the home. It has a rubber cup-like shape and a wooden handle and is used to clear clogs in sinks, tubs, and showers. Do not use this plunger for clearing toilet clogs; that requires a specially shaped plunger called a flange plunger (previous slide). Some flange plungers, though, can be used as standard cup plungers when the flange is tucked up inside.

Plumber's Tape

Plumber's tape is an essential material for preventing leaks at threaded plumbing connections. Often called Teflon tape (although it's not made with Teflon-brand material), plumber's tape is a thin white tape that you wrap around threads on pipes and fittings before twisting the parts together. It adds a bit of lubricant to aid threading and also helps to seal the joint to prevent leaks. Made with PTFE (PolyTetraFluoroEthylene), it is silky in texture and is sold in small rolls.

Channel-Type Pliers

Channel-type pliers are commonly known by the brand name Channel-Locks, and are also known as slip-joint pliers. They're similar to regular adjustable pliers but have extended adjustment sections as well as angled jaws, allowing you to grip pipes or other plumbing parts of almost any size. The long handles provide tremendous leverage for squeezing and twisting. You can use them to grip heavy steel pipe or to gently tighten large plastic nuts on sink drains. If you own only one specialty plumbing tool, this should be the one.

Adjustable Pipe Wrench

An adjustable pipe wrench is the quintessential metal plumbing tool. It provides tremendous leverage and grip. It is designed to grip round objects (such as pipes) securely by digging its sharp serrated teeth into the pipe with increasing pressure as the wrench is turned.

A pipe wrench leaves teeth marks behind and is not recommended for removal of shiny fixtures or for small or fragile pipes, like copper water pipes. Pipe wrenches are primarily used on galvanized steel and iron pipe and on heavy-duty fixtures with rough finishes, such as outdoor spigots or hydrants.

Faucet Valve-Seat Wrench

A faucet valve-seat wrench is a simple tool used to remove the valve seats on a compression faucet. Compression faucets, the oldest style of faucet, work by compressing a rubber washer against a valve seat in the faucet body.

When the washer wears out, the valve seat can become damaged and rough, preventing a complete seal. When that happens, you can remove the valve seat and replace it, using a valve seat wrench. If the seat is not removable, you must regrind it to a smooth surface using a reseating tool.

Faucet Packing, Washers and O-rings

Faucet packing and rubber washers and O-rings are lifesavers for fixing leaky valves on sinks, radiators, and other old or traditional equipment. Packing is a graphite- or wax-coated string that you wrap around valve stems and pack under packing nuts to create a watertight seal. Rubber washers and O-rings are sold in variety packs containing several different shapes and sizes. If you're fixing an old faucet and can't find an official replacement part at the store, a variety pack well have the part you need. It's handy to have one around because it might save you a trip to the store.

Tubing Cutter

The tubing cutter is an essential plumbing tool if you're working with copper pipe. Copper requires clean, square cuts, and tubing cutters do just that—with much less effort than a hacksaw. It has a thin cutting wheel that cuts the metal and a flat pressure wheel that applies pressure when you turn the tool's knob. Clamp the tool onto a pipe and rotate it around the pipe, tightening the knob after every two or three rotations. The cutting wheels gradually cut through the material.

After making the cut, remove the burr on the inside of the pipe, using the de-burring tool (a triangular metal piece) that is fitted to the body of the tubing cutter.

Main Types of Plumbing Pipes Used in Homes

Whether hiring a plumber or taking on a do-it-yourself plumbing project, the experience can be confusing because of the choice of several types of plumbing pipes. Eventually, pipes' uses tend to blend together. Which type of pipe should be used for water supply, drainage, sewer, and even for the exterior? The answer is not as clear as it may have been in the past when the main pipes of choice were galvanized steel or cast-iron.

PEX Pipe

PEX, or cross-linked polyethylene, pipe is one of the newest and most popular pipes to hit the plumbing market. PEX is used only to supply water. PEX is a pipe that is rigid enough to withstand the pressures of water supply but flexible enough to weave throughout walls, ceilings, basements, and crawlspaces. PEX has truly delivered water-supply plumbing into the hands of do-it-yourselfers and professional plumbers.

Pros

• Color-coded red for hot water and blue for cold water

• Highly flexible, with 90-degree curves possible

• Attaches with push-fit plumbing fittings, among other types

• Inexpensive

• Able to join with copper pipe

• Cuts easily

Cons

• Long-term capabilities untested

• May leak with push-fit plumbing fittings

• Cannot be recycled

PVC Pipe

PVC, or polyvinyl chloride, pipe is a drain or vent line type of plumbing pipe. PVC initially gained popularity because it was lighter and easier to work with than traditional galvanized steel pipe. PVC pipe is moderately easy to install and requires little more than a hacksaw and a miter box to cut. PVC glues together with solvents.

Pros

- Diameters clearly marked on the white surface of the pipe

- Inexpensive and can be used for long runs such as for irrigation

- Easier to work with than steel or copper

Cons

- The pipe cannot be unjoined and must be cut

- Glued pipes can be prone to leaking

- Degrades in sunlight

Rigid Copper Pipe

Rigid copper is often used for water supply lines within the home. Rigid copper is easily cut with a hacksaw or with a special copper tube cutter. The connection is a different matter, as it requires a practiced hand to solder copper pipe together. Rigid copper pipe is great for water supply because it does not come with any health risks.

Pros

- Though it is called rigid, this pipe can be slightly bent

- Handles heat well

- Stands up against intense pressures

- Easy to recycle and waste copper pipe even has monetary value

Cons

- Difficult for do-it-yourselfers to work with due to soldered connections

- Expensive

- Develops pinhole leaks

- Inside of pipe may eventually corrode and impede water flow

ABS Pipe

ABS (acrylonitrile butadiene styrene) pipe is mainly used as a vent and drain line. ABS pipe looks very much like PVC pipe, except that it is black and slightly softer.

Pros

- Stronger than PVC pipes

- Good for underground exterior use

- Works well in cold temperatures

Cons

- Often not permitted by building code

- Warps and deforms at certain temperatures.

Flexible Copper Pipe

Flexible copper pipe or tubing is used for final runs to water heaters, refrigerators, and some sinks. Flexible copper is used only for short runs and can be cut with ease with a hacksaw. It can be bent to fit around corners.

Pros

- Fits in tight, unusually shaped areas

- High heat tolerance

Cons

- Expensive

- Thin and prone to breaking

Galvanized Steel Pipe and Cast Iron

Two additional types of pipe are sometimes found in older homes and are infrequently installed, especially by do-it-yourselfers: steel and cast iron pipe.

Galvanized steel pipe was used for decades for drainage, water supply, gas supply, and any number of other purposes. While galvanized steel pipe is still around (particularly for gas supply) it is far less used and is never used for water supply in new construction or remodel projects. Each end of the pipe is threaded, and individual pipes are screwed into each other with connecting joints.

Cast iron pipe was often used for sewer and other drainage purposes. Cast iron pipe is still found in many homes. Cast iron pipe is viable until the point that it rusts completely through. Cast iron is very heavy and difficult to cut. Retrofits tend to replace cast iron pipe with rigid plastic pipes such as ABS.

Pros

• Galvanized steel pipe has the advantage of being extremely strong.

Cons

• Galvanized steel pipe eventually corrodes and blocks water flow.

• Some galvanized steel pipe may pass lead into the water supply.

CHAPTER TWO

Common Plumbing Problems and How to Fix Them

There are many different plumbing problems that can spring up in the average home. Some plumbing problems are more common that others. Some of the most common plumbing problems are also quite easy to fix. Doing the repairs for these common plumbing problems yourself can save you some money.

Low Water Pressure

When someone complains about having low water pressure it is usually at the sink faucet. The first thing to check is if the low water pressure is affecting both the hot and cold water. If both the hot and cold have low pressure the most likely cause is the aerator. Calcium deposits slowly build up in the faucet aerator and reduce the water pressure. A blocked aerator is a very easy thing to fix. To clean out a faucet aerator carefully remove the aerator, clean out any debris and build up on it and put it back on.

Slow Draining Sink

A sink that is draining slowly is a very common plumbing problem. Often the pop-up that is used to stop up the sink can collect a lot of hair and debris over time. To get the drain flowing smoothly again the debris needs to be cleaned out. One way to do this is to use the Zip-it, a handy plumbing tool, to clean out the drain. Another option is to remove the pop-up and clean it out. Most pop-ups are held in place with a nut attached to the drain just under the sink and can be unscrewed by hand or with pliers. Once the nut is removed the pop up can be cleaned and then reinstalled.

Slow Draining Tub

A slow draining tub is another very common plumbing problem that can be easily fixed. Often the tub drain is full of hair which slows the water down as it drains out of the tub. Once again the Zip-it tool or a pair of needle nose pliers are great tools that can be used to reach in and clear out the debris in the drain. If there is a tub stopper in the drain you may have to remove the tub stopper before getting to the hair clog. It is a good idea to clear out the debris in the tub drain on a regular basis even if the tub is not draining slowly. If it is left too long it could end up clogging the drain completely.

Running Toilet

Another common plumbing problem that many people are familiar with is a running toilet. There are various things that can be causing the toilet to run but they are easy to fix. The first step is to figure out what is the cause of the running toilet. Once you know which of the working parts of the toilet is causing the problem you can replace it or repair it and stop the running water.

A jammed garbage disposal is high on the list of common plumbing problems. Many people lose the nifty key that comes with the garbage disposal to help unjam it. Fortunately, an Allen wrench can be used to unjam a garbage disposal. At the very bottom of the disposal there is an opening to insert the key. Using a 1/4 inch Allen wrench simply turn in both directions to free the motor.

Tips for Planning New Plumbing Routes

Any significant plumbing renovation job may require you to run new plumbing lines—whether this means replacing old pipes or running new ones for the first time. The first step in this kind of project is deciding where to run the pipes. This is often easier said than done because pipes will usually be concealed in wall spaces and covered by finished surfaces.

Two Common Ways to Run Plumbing

Most often it is easiest to simply run new pipes in the same cavities that contained the old plumbing. These spaces are already designed to allow for long, unbroken runs for pipes. When using modern plumbing materials, such as PEX tubing that is flexible, this is often the best choice.

If the new plumbing plans call for changes in the fixture layout, it may be easier to run them up from the basement (if you have one). For example, instead of running a bathtub drain over floor joists, the drain line can be dropped into the basement and connected to the main drain line beneath the joists.

Note: It is never advisable to notch out or cut into floor joists or support beams, as this may weaken the structural integrity of the building. Check with local building codes to determine the proper route for tackling any issues with support beams.

Alternative Ways to Run New Plumbing

These are additional ways to run new plumbing in your home. Remember, it's always easier to work in open spaces than in tight spots inside walls. And if you are ever uncertain about the legitimacy of a plumbing plan, check with local inspectors and city officials to ensure that everything you planned will be up to code.

Building a Wall Chase

A chase is a false wall that creates a cavity used to conceal plumbing. The chase can be stacked from floor-to-floor of the home. This allows plumbing to run from the basement to the attic. The chase is most commonly used for running new vent stacks. Similar to the chase is the soffit. Instead of running from floor-to-ceiling, a soffit runs across the top of a wall. Inside pipes can be run vertically to accommodate new plumbing.

Convert an Unused Laundry Chute

An unobstructed, unused laundry chute is perfect for running new pipes. They often run through most of the floors, usually terminating in the basement where connections are easier to make. The chute door can also be left intact and used as an access panel for shut-off valves.

Probing Wall Cavities

A long piece of pipe can be used to check prospective plumbing routes for any obstructions. Once the route is determined to be adequate, the pipe can serve as a guide for running larger- diameter plumbing. This is easily done by sliding the larger pipe over the guide pipe.

Useful Plumbing Tips for Beginners

Are you ready to become a DIY plumbing expert, or at least someone who can fix the minor plumbing issues that come up? You could save many hundreds of dollars by taking care of dripping faucets or overflowing toilets yourself. Take care of minor plumbing problems before they become something only professionals can solve.

We've got six useful tips that you can apply to your plumbing problems as soon as you have the right tools. You may be reluctant to tackle tough plumbing projects alone, but small clogs and leaks can often be fixed without calling in the professionals. It's a good idea to have a plumber's number on hand just in case you encounter an issue you can't solve. Hopefully, you will likely find that minor plumbing projects are easy and satisfying to work on by yourself.

Don't Be Afraid to Replace Parts Inside Your Toilet or Faucet

Taking apart pipes under your sink or shower can lead to messy issues if you make a mistake. However, there's very little you can damage by trying to replace your toilet's flapper or your faucet's cartridge.

Worn flappers are a common cause of leaks between the toilet tank and bowl, and they only cost a few dollars! As a bonus, the package comes with easy-to-follow instructions for replacement.

Most modern faucets can be repaired by replacing the entire interior with a new cartridge. This only requires that you remove a screw or two. So, if you hear the toilet running frequently, or your sink is dripping, get replacement parts and give it a go.

Remove Clogs Without Chemicals

Next time your drain is clearing slowly, don't buy expensive, chemical drain cleaners. Manually unclog a drain with a drain snake. Just insert into the drain and pull back out with (hopefully) the clog culprit attached. If you don't have or don't want to hassle with one, try using a wet/dry shop vacuum to suck out the clog.

Check Your Showerhead for Issues

Thread tape is also one of the easiest ways to fix a dripping showerhead. Chances are, the leak means the threads aren't connecting tightly. Unscrew the showerhead, apply new tape by wrapping in a clockwise direction, and re-attach to stop the drip.

If the showerhead is clogged, soak it in a bowl with warm water and vinegar for about an hour. Use a small brush to loosen any mineral deposits that could be causing blockages in the spray.

Forget Thread Sealing Compounds—Use Thread Tape

Thread sealing compound, commonly known as "pipe dope," can drip and smear. For most DIY projects involving pipe threads around the house, thread tape will work just as well or better. You can buy a multi-purpose tape, which is usually white. Thicker tape is usually yellow for gas or pink for water. Try one of the thicker options for easier handling.

When you wrap the tape, roll it counterclockwise around the threads. Can't get the roll into a tight space? Wrap a few turns of tape around a cheap pen and apply from that. You'll want to wrap your tape around the pipe threads roughly three times for best results.

Use Heat to Loosen Tough Water Pipe Fittings

Can't get that trap under the sink or pipe fitting loose, no matter how hard you try with a pipe wrench? Hardened fittings make it nearly impossible to budge the fitting with brute strength.

You might be able to apply heat to loosen up old, solidified pipe dope. A small propane torch will do the trick, but you'll have to apply heat for a few minutes before much progress can be made. Use heat-resistant material to protect nearby walls.

It may seem obvious, but only heat on metal water pipes, never on or next to gas pipes, and not on plastic pipes or fittings.

Make Your Water Heater More Efficient

Check your water heater's thermostat to make sure it's not set too high. You should be able to go down to 115 degrees and still have enough hot water for your needs. You'll also want to insulate your water heater's tank. Hot water will stay hot longer this way—but be careful not to cover the thermostat. Some utilities provide inexpensive or free insulating blankets that are simple to install.

You may live in an area where sediment collects quickly in the lines. Sediment can also collect quickly in systems using a well. Get rid of the grit by draining a quart of water from your tank once every 3 months. First, turn off the water heater and open the drain into a steel bowl or bucket. This will remove a lot of the sediment that has settled near the bottom of the tank which can make your water heater run less efficiently.

How to Turn off the Water for Plumbing Repairs

Shutting off the water supply in your home is usually necessary when you are making plumbing repairs to any of the fixtures or pipes in your home's plumbing system. There are at least three different places you can shut off the water, and your choice of locations will depend on where the leak or the plumbing repair needs to occur.

Generally, it will require no tools at all to simply shutting off the water.

<u>Here are several locations where water can be shut off, and how to choose the right one.</u>

Turning the Water off at the Fixture or Appliance

If a faucet is dripping or a toilet is running—or if a leak develops in a refrigerator ice maker, dishwasher, washing machine, or any appliance supplied by water—your first and best choice is to shut off the water right at that fixture or appliance. By shutting the water off locally in this way, other fixtures in your house can continue to operate unaffected while you take your time to make the repair.

The fixture shut-off valves will differ in appearance and location, but generally, they will be very close to the fixture or appliance.

• For sink faucets, look for the shutoff valves located below the sink, near where the water supply tubes run up to the tailpieces on the faucet. Any faucet that supplies both hot and cold water will have two valves—one for the hot water supply and one for the cold.

• For toilets, there will be a single shut-off valve (a toilet uses only cold water), usually located near the floor below the water supply valve on the bottom of the toilet tank. This supply valve is usually near the bottom left side of the toilet tank.

• For showers/tubs, look around the tub or shower for an access panel. It may be on the other side of the wall from the tub or shower. If it is not found behind an access panel, then it may be located under the floor in the basement or a ceiling access panel in the floor below.

• For dishwashers, the water supply tube running to the dishwasher often has a fixture shutoff valve controlling it. In many cases, this is also located under the kitchen sink base cabinet, and it may be near the sink faucet shut-off valves.

• For refrigerator ice makers/water dispensers, the small copper or mesh supply tube running to the refrigerator usually has a small saddle valve or fixture shutoff valve that can be shut off to close down the water supply. In some cases, the supply tube running to the refrigerator may tap into a water supply line beneath the sink, near where the sink faucet supply tubes are attached.

• For clothes washers, there is most often a water supply valve controlling the hot water inlet hose and another controlling the cold water. These may be located on a utility sink if your laundry has one, sometimes in a recessed water supply valve box set into the wall near the washing machine. This can be turned off whenever you need to work on the washing machine.

You get the idea. Any fixture or appliance should be equipped with some local shut-off valves.

But if you don't find the shut-off valves, don't worry. You can shut off the water by turning off the main water supply valve near the water meter. That location is described below.

Some homes are equipped with branch valves that can be used to shut off the water supply to selected branch lines in the home. These valves will be located along the main branch pipes and are located in accessible utility areas. For example, water pipes feeding outdoor hose faucets are very often controlled by in-line valves that control only the pipes running to the outdoor faucets.

Turning the Water off at the Water Heater

When a hot water pipe is leaking, or if you need to repair or replace a water heater, there are shut-off valves located near your water heater.

A water heater has two shut-off valves. A cold water inlet valve (often identified by a blue handle) feeds cold water from the main supply into the water heater. This is the valve to shut off if you need to repair or replace the water heater.

The hot water outlet pipe also has a valve that will shut down all hot water leaving the water heater. You can shut off this valve if you have a leak in a hot water pipe somewhere in the house since this valve effectively controls all hot water in the home. Often, this valve is coded with a red handle to indicate it controls hot water. This convenient color coding is important, because often the cold water inlet pipe and the hot water outlet pipe are often very close to one another, and they would be hard to tell apart without this color coding.

Turning the Water Off at the Main Shutoff Valve

If your leak is somewhere in the main branch line, or if there is no fixture shut-off valve near the fixture you need to repair or replace, find the main shut-off valve for the home. This is usually found in a utility space near where the main water line enters the house, or on an outside wall near the water meter. This valve will always be located on the house-side of the water meter and it is usually a rather large valve.

This valve rarely gets closed, so it may be a little stiff to operate.

After shutting off the main shut-off valve, if you open the lowest faucet in your home (such as in a basement or a foundation-level outdoor faucet) and also the highest faucet in the home, it will allow water standing in the plumbing system to drain away. This means the water supply pipes will be empty of water, which can prevent water from spilling out when you begin your work on them.

Turning the Water off at the Water Meter

Finally, you may also be able to shut off the water at the water meter itself. Water meter boxes sometimes have two shutoff valves, one on the customer side and one on the city side of the meter. This should be a last resort, because in many communities there are ordinances that frown on homeowners touching any part of the plumbing system positioned on the street side of the water meter. The plumbing lines beyond the meter technically belong to the city, so you should not touch this valve unless there is no other option—such as if the main shut-off valve on the house side is non-existent or doesn't work.

How to Drain Your Home's Plumbing System

Although not a common task, draining your home's plumbing pipes is occasionally necessary. Some common reasons for doing this include:

• Fixing a water hammer problem.

• Shutting down a seasonal property for the winter.

• To make major plumbing repairs, like replacing or extending the main plumbing lines.

Water Hammer

Water hammer (also called hydraulic shock) is a situation in which plumbing pipes bang loudly when faucets are turned on and off, or when an appliance suddenly starts or stops the flow of water. The problem occurs because of air in the plumbing lines, which allow the water to oscillate back and forth and bang the pipes against one another or against the wood framing. Even if your system has air chambers to absorb this shock, too much air trapped in the system will make the problem persist. The answer is to drain the system and refill it so the air gaps are confined to the designated air chambers.

Seasonal Shutdown

Draining the plumbing pipes is one of many items on a winter preparation checklist. These are especially important when a property in a cold climate will be left unattended for the winter since frozen pipes that burst can fill an empty home with thousands of gallons of water and cause many thousands of dollars in damages.

Major Plumbing Repairs

Although draining the entire system is not part of every major repair or addition to the home plumbing system, it can sometimes be necessary, such as when a basement bathroom is being installed, and the plumbing pipes lying above the installation need to be drained when the new pipes are connected to the existing system. There can be a substantial amount of water in the supply pipes within the home, and at the moment the pipes are cut in order to connect the new supply pipes, this water can flow out unless they have first been drained.

Draining your home's water supply pipes, and refilling them when the work is done, is a very easy process.

What You'll Need

Equipment / Tools

• Tubs and faucets

Instructions

1. Shut Off Water Valve

Shut off the main water valve at the water meter.

2. Open Sink Faucets

Starting at the top floor, open all the sink faucets. the will allow air into the system, which will help the flow of water as you drain the system.

3. Open Faucet in Laundry Tub

Go to the basement or the lowest level in your home, then open the faucet in your laundry tub or lowest sink, and let all the water from the above floors drain out.

4. Open Tub or Shower Faucets

Now go back upstairs or to the highest level in the home and open the tub/shower faucets.

5. Flush All Toilets

Flush all the toilets, emptying the tanks.

6. Leave Faucets in Open Position

If you are leaving the property unattended (such as when leaving a vacation home for the winter), leave the faucets in an open position.

There should be no water coming out of any faucets, except a possible slight residual drip from the lowest faucet as any remaining water in the pipes dribbles out. You're done!

Tip

When a home is left unattended for a long period, standing water in toilets, sink and tub drain traps and floor drains can evaporate, removing the drain seal that keeps sewer gases from rising up into the home. Some experts recommend blocking drains and toilet bowls with wadded-up cloths or plastic wrap to keep the sewer system sealed off from the house during long absences.

How to Charge With Water

1. Close Basement Faucet

Close the basement faucet or lowest level faucet in the house.

2. Close Upper Faucets

Now close all the upper faucets. Closing the faucets allows air to remain in the pipes to recharge the air chambers you may have in your home's plumbing system.

3. Open Main Water Valve

Go back and open the main water valve to let the water back into your pipes.

4. Turn on Faucets

Now, one by one, starting with the highest level faucets, turn on the faucets and let the air/water sputter out until only clear water flows from the faucet. You may see discolored water come out at first, but this is normal.

5. Open Faucets

Open the shower faucets to let water back into those pipes.

6. Flush Toilets

Flush the toilets to refill the tanks.

Once the water is running clear, turn off the faucets starting at the highest floor level and work your way down through the house. You may have an occasional sputter the next time you use a faucet, but any remaining air will quickly be purged.

Is It Time to Replace Your Home's Plumbing?

Failure of any portion of your home's plumbing can lead to major property damage and loss of furnishings. Piping and pipe connections often fail due to age, lack of maintenance, major fluctuations in temperature, faulty components or low-quality installations. Consider the fact that much of your home's piping is concealed beneath concrete or behind walls. Therefore, knowing the expected life cycle of your plumbing and indications of failure can help any homeowner know when it is time to replace their home's plumbing.

Pipe Material

Assess your home's plumbing to determine what type of piping material is installed in the home. Different materials have different life expectancies and pose different problems. When you purchased your home, an appraisal or inspection report would have detailed the type of piping material in your home. For instance, historic homes used clay, which deteriorates much more quickly than modern materials. Each pipe material has a lifespan:

• Copper: 50+ years

• Brass: 40 to 45 years

• Cast Iron: 75 to 100 years

• Galvanized Steel: 20 to 50 years

• PVC piping can last indefinitely.

While these long-life cycles may look impressive, you also need to consider the pipe joints, fittings and mechanical components that connect your plumbing to household fixtures. Aged or faulty fixtures and compromised connections can lead to leaks and water backups.

Signs of Failing Plumbing

The most obvious sign that your home has a plumbing problem will be obvious pipe cracks, corrosion or leaks from the piping. Other signs will also show plumbing issues: wet baseboards or the area behind dishwasher or sinks, water-stained or warped flooring, and water tubing that is rust-colored can indicate leaking or corroding pipes.

Low water pressure can indicate a clogged drain or a leak downstream from the fixture. A gurgling or rattling sound from your piping may indicate a pipe blockage that is trapping air. An inspection of crawl spaces and enclosed areas for dampness or mold is also an indication of a pipe leaking. Slow-moving drains should always be cleared with a drain cleaner or plumber's "snake," as it indicates a blockage in the pipeline.

Repair or Replace?

Dislodging material in blocked pipes, replacing faulty fixtures and pipe connectors, and even replacing faulty exposed pipes are all projects that don't require a plumber. Keep in mind when the problem is not exposed piping, but concealed underground or behind a wall, be prepared for demolition and floor/wall repairs.

A good rule of thumb is to replace plumbing when you renovate your kitchen, bathroom or basement. You can keep the cost low by replacing only the exposed piping if no other sign of leaking water is present. However, if walls will be removed, inspect hidden pipes and joints to determine if they should be fixed or replaced. Just in case your project leads to a more complicated situation, keep a good plumber's contact information handy.

Household Plumbing Inspection Checklist

When plumbing problems erupt suddenly, they can do so with a severity that borders on the catastrophic. But a regular inspection of your key plumbing fixtures can help you spot and correct developing problems before they become such emergencies.

Predictably, the places where you should focus your inspection checklist are those rooms where there are many plumbing fixtures—the bathroom and kitchen. But don't forget to check around the house for the other appliances and fixtures, ranging from the hose spigots outside the house to the water heater in the basement or utility area.

Bathroom

Bathrooms get lots of use by every member of the family, and it's no surprise that this is the room most likely to see plumbing problems.

• **Faucets. It** is the sink, tub, and shower faucets that most often need attention in a bathroom. Check them regularly for leaks. Replace bad washers or cartridges to remedy dripping faucets. Water supply lines hidden in the walls for tub and shower drains can be especially problematic since such hidden leaks can cause major damage before you even spot it. Hidden water pipe leaks often reveal themselves with signs of water damage in the room below the plumbing pipes. Watch the operation of faucets as you run the water—if you notice weak water pressure or an irregular spray pattern, it may be because there is calcium buildup on the aerator. Aerators can be removed and cleaned manually, or calcium buildup can be removed by soaking in vinegar.

• **Drains.** Tub, shower, and sink drains in a bathroom are especially prone to soap and hair clogs, and rather than waiting for these to become full blockages, you should periodically disassemble drain traps and remove hair and debris. At the same time, it's a good idea to snake out the branch drains to remove clogs before they become full blockages.

• **Toilets.** A toilet has many working parts, and any one of them can wear down and cause problems. Remove the tank lid on the toilet and watch what happens as you flush it. A toilet that continues to run rather than shutting off at the end of the flush cycle is wasting a lot of water. Fixing a running toilet is often remarkably easy. If your toilet rocks slightly when you sit on it, or if you notice water seeping around its base, then it is likely that the wax ring that seals the toilet base to the drain opening has worn out and needs to be replaced.

• **Caulk seals.** Although the caulk around tubs and showers is not actually "plumbing," when caulking fails, it can allow water from a bathtub or shower to get behind walls and under floors, and the resulting water damage can be catastrophic. Periodically check all caulk beads along floors and walls to make sure it is intact. Seal any gaps you find with fresh caulk. Every few years, it is a good idea to remove the old caulk and apply a new bead of high-quality silicone tub-and-shower caulk.

Kitchen

The kitchen is another room heavy with plumbing fixtures. At least twice a year, inspect all the fixtures and fix any problems you find.

• **Sink drains.** The kitchen sink gets lots of use, and a sink strainer is a common place where leaking can occur. Watch the strainer area and the P-trap as water in the sink drains out. P-trap fittings may need to be tightened, and the strainer basket should be replaced when it begins to leak or becomes corroded. A sink that drains too slowly may have a clog building in the P-trap or branch drain; these fittings can be disassembled and cleaned out. Clean the kitchen sink drain occasionally. Using a mild homemade drain cleaner through your kitchen sink drain regularly will help to break up the usual buildup in the drain and keep the water flowing.

• **Faucets.** A leaky kitchen faucet is the single most common plumbing repair there is, and it can quietly waste hundreds of gallons of water each year. Watch your faucet carefully as you operate the lever, and repair the faucet if it requires it.

• **Shutoff valves.** The fixture shutoff valves that control the water supply to the sink faucet, dishwasher, and refrigerator water lines are intended to completely shut off the flow of water when they are closed. During your inspection, close the valves tightly and make sure they operate as intended. If they do not shut off the water completely, they should be replaced.

• **Garbage disposer.** Problems with garbage disposers usually are found in the drain connections where a dishwasher discharge connects to the disposer, or where the disposer discharge runs to the sink drain. Inspect these points and tighten the connections or replace the gaskets if they show signs of leaking. A garbage disposer that has a foul smell should be cleaned. Follow the manufacturer's advice for routine maintenance of the garbage disposal.

• **Dishwasher.** During your inspection tour, take a few minutes to watch and listen to the dishwasher in action. A dishwasher that is slow to fill may have a problem with the water supply hose or the shutoff valve that controls it. If the dishwasher is slow to drain, or if drain water remains in the bottom of the dishwasher after the cycle is over, inspect the water discharge hose for clogs or pinching.

• **Refrigerator.** A refrigerator with a water dispenser and icemaker should have its filter replaced regularly—most manufacturers recommend twice each year. A clogged filter can block water flow to the dispenser or icemaker. Also, check the water supply hose for signs of wear; replace it if necessary.

Septic and Sewer

A stoppage in the main sewer line or septic system is a very serious plumbing problem and one that poses potential health risks. Regular inspection and maintenance is the best way to prevent this.

• Maintain the septic system. If you have a septic system with a drain field (common in rural areas) avoid problems by having the system inspected and serviced regularly. With a tank system, have the tank pumped out whenever it becomes full. For drainage field systems, make sure your family knows what kinds of materials should not go down the drain. Many experts suggest that you avoid flushing food materials into a septic system. Bleach-based cleaners should also be avoided since these interfere with the biological breakdown of wastes that is essential to a septic system.

• Maintain your sewer main. If your house is served by municipal sewer lines, prevent mainline blockages through regular maintenance. For homes that see periodic stoppages, usually caused by tree roots in the sewer lines, an annual snaking of the line by a professional sewer service will prevent floor drains from backing up into the home. You can evaluate the effectiveness of the sewer line by emptying all sinks and tubs at the same time and seeing if a floor drains back up or if it takes a long time for all the drains to empty. Watch for signs of a pending sewer drain clog and deal with them before they become full-blown stoppages.

• Inspect vent pipes. An integral part of your home's drain and sewer system are the vent pipes that equalize air pressure and vent sewer gases. These pipes usually exit through the top of your roof, and if they become blocked with debris or snow and ice, the drain system in your house will not work as effectively. During your tour of the plumbing system, visually inspect the vent pipes extending through your roof for signs of blockage. You will likely have several of these vent pipes in your roof — one for each main soil stack, and often secondary vent pipes, as well.

Around the House

The bathroom, kitchen, and sewer system are the major plumbing components, but some many other fixtures and appliances should be periodically inspected for problems:

• Water heater. Look for signs of water leaking in the cold water inlet pipe and hot water exit pipe above the water heater. Also, look around the base of the water heater for leaking that may be caused by a faulty temperature and pressure (T and P) relief valve, or a bad drain valve. Every few years, the water heater tank should be flushed to remove sediment from the bottom of the tank. On gas water heaters, the burner unit should occasionally be inspected and cleaned by a professional service person.

• Branch shutoff valves. If your system has shutoff valves that control different zones of the plumbing system, check these to make sure they are operating properly. If you find faulty valves, they should be replaced.

• Sump pump. If your home has a basement with an under-floor drainage system and sump pit, check this to make sure it is operating properly. You can do this by filling the sump pit with water manually and checking to make sure the pump activates to empty the water.

• Outdoor hose spigots. Outdoor faucets often get overlooked, but these, too, can develop leaks and need repair—by replacing washers or cartridges. Outdoor spigots in cold climates can be especially prone to cracking due to extreme winter temperatures; replace any bad spigots you find.

• Irrigation system. Lawn sprinkler systems should be inspected at the start of the watering season to make sure all spray heads are operating properly. And at the end of the watering season, the system should be winterized and drained or blown free of water to prevent freezing and rupture of the pipes over the winter.

• Washing machine. Periodically inspect the water hoses for signs of wear. Rubber hoses that begin to bulge are near the end of their useful lives and should be replaced. Hoses that burst while the owners are away are a major cause of expensive water damage. Also, check the valves that control the hot and cold water hoses for your washing machine. Replace them if they do not completely stop the flow of water when shut off.

• Check home water pressure. Avoid excess stress on your home's plumbing system by making sure the water pressure is at a safe level. It only takes a few minutes to test water pressure with a pressure gauge. If the pressure is too high, then install or repair/replace the pressure regulator to bring it down to a safe level.

CONCLUSION

Water supply is a system of pipes that brings fresh water into the home. The system is highly-dependent of pressure. Water in these pipes come from one of two sources: City water, Wells.

City water enters your house from a humongous pipe 'the main pipe' that's usually parallel to your street. If your connection to the main has a problem, call a professional. Damage to the main can result in civil lawsuits and hefty fines.

People who don't have access to city water usually get their fresh water supply from wells. Water must then be pumped into the home at high pressures. Reduced pressure keeps water from reaching the furthest and highest parts of your house.

Running showers and faucets are usually the first victims of low pressure. Factors affecting pressure range from leaks to blockages. If the leak is caused by a loose connection, it's easily handled in-house.

The main pipe is connected to your water meter. There's a shutoff valve before or after your meter. The valve cuts off the water supply system making it useful when doing repairs.

Correctly installed piping is leak-proof. The system, however, disintegrates with time. In some cases, a plumber may find it necessary to do a complete overhaul of the plumbing.

The water supply system performs optimally when pressure is high. This makes the system rather sensitive to damage.

To illustrate, a leak in the drainage system will only cause damp-related problems. By contrast, leaks in the water supply system take things a step further: They affect water pressure. Low pressure makes it impossible to run showers and flush toilets.

Evidently, leaks are most harmful in the water supply system. Due to the sensitivity of the system, its problems are best handled by professionals.

Plumbing makes or breaks a house. Maintaining the plumbing keeps a house's value high. Therefore, professional plumbing services must be part of a house maintenance's schedule.

Good plumbing efforts also keep the house free of allergenic mold. Most people only find out about their mold problem when they are selling the house. Considering the health risks posed by these molds, that's a saddening fact. Prioritize your plumbing.